C0-APK-298

SUDDEN THAW

PEGGY O'BRIEN

SUDDEN THAW

Orchises 2004 Washington

Copyright © 2004 Peggy O'Brien

Library of Congress Cataloging-in-Publication Data

O'Brien, Peggy, 1945-
    Sudden thaw / Peggy O'Brien.
    p. cm.
    ISBN 0-914061-99-2 (alk. paper)
    I. Title.

PS3615.B763S83 2004
811'.6—dc21

                                    2003056465

ACKNOWLEDGEMENTS

"Transgression" (VI) from "Ruth" was published by *The Irish Press;* "Master and Servant" (IX) by the *Southwest Review;* and "Gleaning among the Sheaves" (XII) by *Cyphers.* Parts I, II, III, IX, XI, XV, XVII, and XXI of "Annaghmakerrig" were published by *Eire-Ireland;* and III appeared as "Virtual Reality" in *The Yale Review.* "Bullheads" was titled "Fishing Together" when it came out in the *Yale Anglers' Journal.* "Dreamers" appeared in *Ravishing Disunities* (edited by Agha Shahid Ali). "Hospital Sonnets" (I) was published as "The Beast" by *The Formalist.* "Invisible Mending" was published by *The American Scholar.*

Design: Rachel Lathbury

Cover painting: *Home at Montclair* by George Inness (1893)
Courtesy of the Sterling and Francine Clark Art Institute
Williamstown, Massachusetts, USA

Manufactured in the United States of America

ORCHISES PRESS
P.O. Box 20602
Alexandria, VA 22320-1602
G 6 E 4 C 2 A

To the memory of my parents,

RICHARD J. AND RUTH J. O'BRIEN

TABLE OF CONTENTS

SUDDEN THAW

PART ONE

HOSPITAL SONNETS

I

Visiting you sick I am your guest.
The big occasion is a party, tea
Al fresco in the garden. I wear a hat.
I speak in gloves. I wouldn't dare to eat
Since you've become polite. Your enemy
Behind the shutters has unearthly vision,
Sees each bony finger crooked and every
Drop that drains your eyes to pale, patrician
Blue. The beast's subduing you. We can't
Have that. I need to feed you peasant fare,
Spuds and meat, shove them down your gullet;
But I bring you grapes and brie and fear
I'll give myself. I see his haunches shudder
As he eats you whole. He has no manners.

II

I hit the mall before the hospital,
I did. I had to have those fancy creams.
I had to make myself invulnerable
To face you, something way beyond my means,
Your flesh in tears, your lips hung up to dry,
Your bones a trellis for your rambling pain,
That look you looked at me, your washed out blue eyes
Beach glass begging on the ocean's margin
To go home. I rub the narcissism
In each night, then change and go to bed,
Lay still and sleek, an animal within
The underbrush, the hunter stalked by dread.
The mirror won't smile back at me. It swallows
Kisses on your cheek into a hollow.

III

I never thought I'd see it like this, the sky
Accused by dead men's skinny fingers, or
Our sweet placenta planet hanging by
The thin threads of birches rooting air.
You weighed in Christmas day fat as a turkey.
I checked the photograph. You filled a chair.
Today, you nod your head agnostically,
Questions blowing your mind, icing your hair,
You who had all the answers. Even my dear
Fatherly hills recede in front of my eyes
Like abstract blotting paper props, a series,
Flats the players fill out with their lines.
You're leaving faster than the snow is melting.
I live in absence now. You're not yourself.

IV

There is a pain so innocent it takes
You back and not your breath away, an ingrown
Irritant whose charm it is to nag and make
Life miserable and ignorant and long.
It makes you strut, the non-believer gone
To church, the healthy visiting the sick,
A tragedy in black and white with popcorn,
Dying of a cold, complaints like mink.
And then there's your pain, so grown-up you daren't
Think its name. Say ah or something not just
Silence shrouding like your skin the prayer
Within that levitates as whispered dust.
A holy man for you now food is pain.
Your only words are never, never again.

V

Of course these are for me and not for you.
You are the occasion not the agent.
It's the way to keep the boundary true
Like ice. Our motives have to be transparent,
As the ice storm was an inventory
Making every item count beneath
Museum glass, letting twigs enjoy
Their twigness, so the needles, grass and leaves,
The general shimmer and the isolation
Of the dying in their cubicles.
I need to see you. We all must be seen.
I pray my pen may write like icicles
Whose weeping makes them sharper. May the crisis
Of the thaw release the poem's grace.

VI

Your wife, my mother, who can still appall
Admits she swears each morning at the kitchen
Sink, cursing the Lord. I am a crystal
Tree and something's shattered concentration
Racing like a lunatic along a limb,
To think that there are other options: cracking,
Crying, cursing, heresy within
My reach, if I weren't rooted in your static
Sadness. I absorbed and soon I'll flower
You as though there were no other way.
I long ago eschewed my Faustian
Extremes, preferring natural displays.
But I am broken now, chrysalides
From some experiment beneath a tree.

VII

To have left and then be back again,
Each notch along the route a splice of time
Unrolling like the truth of your condition,
Diagnosis winter, a matter of time.
This is where we lived. Dilapidated
Triple deckers, shingles, stoops and sloping
Porches. It is summer. I am fat.
My mother's yelling. You are in the shop.
This is the old road to Springfield on the other
Side of the river. Night. The road is glare
Ice. I still may die before you. Specters
Duplicate their flame-life on the water's
Surface, reaching out across it. Flickers.
Stationary. Memory in the river.

VIII

You're the center of an energy
We rarely see except up close or far
Away and ordinarily we need
An instrument to chart a flower or a star.
Yesterday the news was big. A quark,
The top quark (up, down, bottom, charm and strange),
Was found, so heavy it may light the dark,
The petals of the universe explained.
And you we heard are dying fast, so fast
Our grief is awe; but no one's told us why,
Except a thing is living in you drastic
As a rose unfolding to the sky.
Enough I'd thought. I want the winter through.
Now literally I see it taking you.

IX

They make them hard and shiny so as not
To be the earth, the risks and germs contained,
The euphemisms closing by remote
Control behind you in the next domain.
A waiting room, the surgeon drops his mask
To offer words so frank they are the flesh,
My father's liver. Then the doctor asks
With tactful eyes if we have any questions.
Yes, I wonder would you mind my diving
In? I'd like a swim inside your blue-green
Chlorine gown. You see, my father's dying,
I'm alone. I feel about fifteen.
Words, just words, like tissue they weren't able
To sew up. His word was "friable."

X

Language is as far from you as hope.
Everything that half exists, the blue
We count on, trust like breath itself, the snow,
The names that melt, expire, fade, the truth.
Bloodwork sounds like homework, housework, honest
Labor not the pathological
Enumerating of innate resistance,
Fighting breath by breath, cell by cell,
The struggle for each morsel of the common
Portion. It is March. The river's free
To be itself. The ice is writing home,
In loops. Its loose limbed, fluid gait and easy
Air are you. It is your signature
Seen from on high, some scribble about cancer.

XI

I can't help it. You are Christ restrained
And parched in need of swabbing with a sponge,
Your face eroded like a great Cézanne,
Its planes a prayer to structure under mountains
Of distraction. You were concentrating.
Master of the monosyllable
In life, you are a minimalist of pain,
Each breath a hard and priceless jewel.
Forgive me all of this, this lapse from common
Sense. You'd set me straight if you weren't sick,
Too sick for speech, but, Dad, our planet seen
From space is radiant. We are aesthetic.
When I left the hospital at dawn
The air was air, like nothing I had ever known.

INSOMNIA

My alarm clock is gasping for air.
One by one the minutes bob up
To the surface. 3 AM.
I'm looking through a telescope
But in. Stars littering the dark
Like bogcotton. Minnows darting
For the bottom leave the faintest
Trace. I recognize that glassy stare.

I could walk home easily
From here. Step by step, star
By star, stone by shining stone,
Ford the river. Finally, my body
Is a petal wafting down
A well, side to side, an echo
Disappearing as it breathes, falling
Asleep at last, assumed weightless.

ALTERATIONS

I'm almost ashamed to say it:
My father liked to sew.
He'd lend a hand from time
To time to the tailor, and more.

By day he made important
Alterations, a shoulder
Tucked, a cuff turned up,
A waist nipped neatly in.

At night, however, he mended,
Turned inside out his common
Art for us, his "girls,"
Made feminine adjustments.

He seemed to like the smallness,
Retractile in the shop,
Beneath the kitchen lamp,
A corner of himself.

Separate and safe until the day
I barged into the bathroom
And saw this long, red,
Thick needle on him.

The breach between us was
Irreparable. I was
It seemed my mother, breasts
And blood and shameful places.

They entered him the winter
That he finally fell
Apart. An elegant Indian
Surgeon stitched him up.

My father lay in bed,
Piecing it together,
Unpicking sins, rejoining
Seams, impossibly frayed.

One day like Prospero
He rose and leaned upon
His intravenous feeder
To go to the bathroom, alone.

His johnnycoat flew open
As he passed. I saw
His freckled back, heron
Legs and shrunken buttocks.

Something tore again.
I felt it as I pulled
Away in haste, something
Even he can't mend.

BULLHEADS

We are floating
On an afternoon as wide and calm
As Norwich Lake the way
I choose to see it.
I am reading to your breathing.
I am perched on the end of your hospital bed,
The stern again,
Slipping virginally into Henry James's final
Work. I am relaxed, alert
The way you were
Then yielding to the rhythm
Of a syntax that is time,
Anfractuosities the sense we make of it,
Fishing for meanings.

Bullheads. You were after bullheads, snouting
Evil at the bottom of the lake,
Their dreaded leers and horns and bulging
Eyes, their cudgel skulls,
Slitherings through nightmare, in
And out of weeds down there as thin as hair or
Fishing line,
The bait an even greater
Abomination I could not pick up or
Hook for fear of being
Hooked and sucked
Senseless.

Antics to distract a god
Or angler with no sons. They didn't anger
You who left me to my own devices,
Surreptitiously undressing
My lunch,
The brown paper folds,

The wax-paper zips,
Parting the lips of sandwiches,
My pudgy hand no stranger then to secrets,
Tearing the too soft, manufactured flesh
Of cold cuts,
Slipping a bit onto a hook,
Then watching the wedge of violently
Pink meat oscillate,
A shred of panty or of private skin,
A lure for girlish perch on recess
Just beneath the surface
Where the sun reached,
Kissing each inimitable speckle.

I am squeamish still,
Especially where you're concerned,
Leaving the room
Before the nurse's expert hypodermic arc
Punctures your arm,
Before a catheter's inserted.
Whenever a new fishgut tube is introduced,
I vanish to the corridor
The way omnisciently you'd row us
From the water when a storm was brewing.
Sitting on our separate rocks,
Avoiding the lee of trees, each other's eyes,
We'd watch the Sistine show,
Adamic flashes,
All the scars I'd ever know,
Prophesied across the wide open sky,
While I would hunch into my wet, pubescent chest,
My two tiny breasts electrified.

And then the peace again returning
To the fishing, dropping
Hope in one place, waiting,

Rowing to another, the sound
Of oarlocks like your breath,
The clock that counts our time
Together,
My finger in the water even then
Slicing as my pen does now memory,
The surface instantly repairing,
Static point within the moving wheel.

Driving home I see peripherally
A stickman on the ice
Ice fishing,
The hole that must be there,
Your head against the bedsheet.
You are sinking to a place I cannot see.
The thaw this year here has been sudden.
Men have vanished
Between words on a page
And we will never know what they were trying to say,
Why they dropped a line into a world
They couldn't see or know
Except by going there.

The Swamp, All Hallows

I must be seeing things in this obscure
Light. Charnel thoughts, for I have thought
Myself into the night behind the mirror,
An element that's natural only not
My own. My father lies in water, turbid
And perfumed, decaying vegetation
And the rot of animals. The solid
Earth is an idea as alien
As non-existence. Air takes root, if needs be, sprouts
And pokes like pain from conversation, bones
Or silver birches each articulate
Though knee-deep in reflection, lost in their own
Thoughts: femur, tibia. I flay
A face with x-ray speed and pessimism
Getting down to facts inevitably
Skeletal, consume the last illusion,
Pick the fish-bone comb of the horizon
Clean of every leaf and then proceed
To slip between the bars. I keep my eyes on
Certain perpendiculars then seep
And stain the way the casuistic squid ink
Of a marsh invades a childish under-
Brush that's never known disease. I think
That this is what they call acceptance, the wonder
Of the sunset dawning through the twilight's eyelid
Swollen by such sobs, pale lavender
And dusty rose, dove and violet,
The thinnest human skin resisting water.

When the agate glass reflects the absence
Of the light, you know you're in for it.
The ghosts appear in negatives like ice
That barely blisters water, passing thoughts
Of doom. It's lurking everywhere exhumed.

I smell the musk of my own fear. The murk
Of five o'clock eats up the eye of home.
I'm hurrying but it's as though a word
Or step has been unwittingly omitted.
Flesh may surface yet, though every tragic
Scratch will still show up, a scar, elisions
Of the seasons, centuries, a logic
Pure and simple. The dialogue of dusk
Ensues. Philosophers are perched. They hoot
Like love-lorn whales from depths their great-winged message
To the world: that things, to wit, are moot.

INVISIBLE MENDING

I used to save them up
For you. A heap
On the bedroom floor
In a corner,
The sordid details
Of my life. Saturday afternoons.
"Bless me, Father,"
And they looked like sins,
A slack-jawed hem,
A zipper
With a jack-o-lantern leer,
A silk blouse
With a gash across its face.
You had the gift then
Of invisibly mending them,
Turning a blind eye
Inside out, and I
The knack of walking on air.

The day they laid you out
I had the task
Of buying you a shirt.
Absurd. I chose
The poshest shop in town
Now that you were out
Of business. The quality. The cost.
That fabric wouldn't last
I heard you mutter,
But look, an extra button
For the journey,
There to fix perhaps
A madly flapping
Cuff at sea.
That ought to keep you busy,

Something for your coffin,
Pushed out like a paper boat
Onto a seamless ocean.

PART TWO

WALKING WITH YO-YO MA

No one hears but me the vast
Pacific rolling solo through
My body, Yo-Yo Ma, Bach's Suite
For Cello Number One. Walking
With my Walkman, the long, coaxing
Bow tickling the taut
Strings, the burnished sternum humming
Moaning, sobbing, choking on the low
Vibrato.

Frost. The Irish sea is numb.
The air is fog embalmed. It's Christmas
And a yellow bathing cap
Bores through the gray the way on certain
Days our sun prevails or one star
Quickens twilight or a stocky
Woman in her middle-age
Can feel the need to feel her flesh
Effervesce.

Thousands of miles west across
The merciless Atlantic things
Are still as they were. A white, silk scarf
Embossed with winter roses
Is flutterless. The mirror holds its breath
Inanimate as nipple tips,
The peaks of gables, pines and pickets
Draped in a galactic
Quiet.

Snow listens infinite
Of pockets like a woman pumped
With music. Ticking, sluicing cease.
Each ripple is a crucial

Alteration in a lover's
Tone of voice. The space becomes
A mouth, each flake a star, each cell
A soul on red alert for the
Crescendo.

THE SAME LANGUAGE

Violett-le-Duc (with two t's) had to be
A pimp, a devotee of beauty living off
The past. And Pippin didn't simply happen to be
Short. Was Innocent an Innocent the III?
And Clovis? Not a pungent spice for ham. Absurd.
He was a butcher with a temper like a mace.
This has to stop. I'm slipping off the Hill of Howth.
I've drained the Irish Sea of sense to see your face.

Abduct me, take me to rebellious Languedoc,
An Albigenses wannabe snug in a Dublin
Pub, smug and passive on the pseudo-blueness
Of Gauloises, opinions and pretensions, words like smoke,
Spiraling and longing for the stake. The plan
Of love is necessarily chaotic, you in
One place, me another. But my head is in Toulouse.
All my life I have been practicing to burn.

I wander through the rhododendron maze of other
People's words, another story, you, your wife,
An afternoon, the hill, her high heels, heather, summer.
I must find a word that's muscular enough
To swim to France. This distance makes me crane my neck
To look for you, hook memory south to Languedoc
To see your ass or arse, whatever, furze or gorse,
Etcetera, a day that made you dirty. Yes.

If I were only with you now in Languedoc
Stretched on your turlough of a bed, we'd talk and talk
Forgetting sudden loss. No one knows when love
Will breath on them a dead language wet with rhyme,
Italicizing the vernacular of time,
A miracle like sight. "Oc," I would say, "oc,"
A vowel and consonant so tightly locked they fuck
Each other speechless until just breathing is enough.

To know the confident assent where yes is no
To language other than your own, articulate
A faith in God's own chosen tongue, be literal
About the hint of cloves inside the rose, know you know
Directions that the nose discovers, follow it
To Languedoc, the village and the street, a place
Where lines are steep but script is straight, the house an "L"
For level like your bed, my image of your face.

I've been nomadic far too long upon the sand
Of languages and nations. I don't even talk like a Yank,
A pure Yank, that is, anymore. Of course I hanker
For a place whose name denotes intransigence.
I tried to dial Languedoc, mistook the code,
And got an anguished "oui, oui, oui," a squawk out of the dark
Of Europe, then dropped a digit and the void
Responded with its pre-recorded robot talk.

I'm not a fool. I long ago gave up on home;
But we may die without a history, which is why I hoard
The facts you offer, intimate, implicit kisses;
But I also know, when so many separate, self-respecting words
Line up and wait their turn, yearn for even half-rhyme
With a word that might mean home, when smoke diffuses,
Drifts, sensuously shifts in air, that reason
Even might be tempted to embrace the sea.

I look across to Bray Head and I want the two
To lock themselves together tight, suck the stone,
With arms and legs like spider prongs; but the aquamarine
Dream beneath me keeps on dreaming out and in
Like new love. A gorse fire blazes on the face of Dalkey
Hill pulsating red messages, alarming passion,
Giving rise to smoke, a meditative gray-blue,
Sketching and resketching futures out across the bay.

That's the way I operate. Better you should know
It now than later. I will always see
Essentially the things I want to see and then correct
Them in my sleep. Languedoc, therefore, to me
Is a long tongue rooted in the Pyrenees
That arches up to take refreshment from the Loire,
Then laps with shameless ardor salt water from a sea
Proverbially blue, transparent as a fact.

The survival of a couple, Provençal, a whale,
May all be providential, equally the absence
Of a butcher in a village, chaste and high
On carnal thoughts where matrons pant for tongue whole
Afternoons spent in the meadows in between their thighs.
The bells high up are tinkling. I can see your woolly
Head. I've pressed behind the glass of memory
A tuft of hair not as a souvenir but evidence.

I've been to Montpellier and Carcassone, seen towers
Conical and comical like talismanic
Wizard hats to keep the infidel
At bay, the Visigoths and me. The Inquisition's
Met and found me guilty. I'm a heretic
At last. I chose to see your beatific smile,
To taste the desert off your skin, to waste entire
Days in bed inquisitive of secrets with my tongue.

I need to lick the inside crevices of sin
And swim in the exotic element of your
Uniqueness, know subacqueous desire. Sick.
It takes a Catholic, lapsed not half enough, to languish
So in mere imaginings, a hypochondriac
To boot. I can imagine anything. I don't imagine,
Though, phone lines grinning. We must listen to the silver
Tongues of fish. We may just speak the same language.

BLIZZARD

I half-expected we would meet today,
Blizzards having been our métier,
The rush out of the blue just when you're certain
It is over, that finally a season
Without memory is in, the shy
Advance of April to a thin-skinned sky,
Not this countenance that frowns power
Down, this yeti loping through the town,
Draped and empty, hushed, the everyday
In chaste abeyance, as though someone were away.

The common snored, the churches clean forgot,
Even the town clock seemed stopped like a heart.
Skittish teacups tremored on their saucers
As the ground heaved to the beat, that old familiar
Tune, that whistle of anticipation:
A man in work boots and a down parka, branding
The snow as he advances to my threshold
In the flesh. I ask him in. The cold
Comes with him, but the sight so magnifies
My memory that heat turns solid ice
To water instantly, as each fragile
Snowflake on each separate bristle melts
In his beard to tears. Sit down. Sit down. And stay.

The storm was our excuse and set the pace,
Coming down as bold as lust, knowing
It would soon be over but coming down
Like angels for a last look at the earth,
Kissing its sweet face. Why not rehearse
Apocalypse, especially when the stage
Is set, the lines and movements pat? Indulge
The easy heresy of loving weather
More than love. Imagine my entire

House embedded, snow up to the eaves,
The two of us cocooned, marooned in sleep,
Groping in an opaque dream, that slow
Motion all we know: snow and more snow.

HYPOTHERMIA

It's when a body can't wait to tear off her clothes,
Despite the fact that technically they're freezing.
When it comes to love, what does anybody know?

Pain and heat make such ideal bedfellows
How are we to know it is our blood seizing
Up, clotting from exposure, ceasing to flow,

Rupturing the trust of capillaries closest
To the surface, wreaking havoc like a kiss?
When it comes to love, what does anybody know?

Nothing makes me hotter than a cold shoulder
Or shower. I manufacture hell, pleasing and pleasing
Whomever until I'm numb, a slave to snow.

We need the sun, yet let us find the glow
Of genuine admiration and it smites our eyes.
When it comes to love, what does anybody know?

Burning up inside the truth remains subzero.
Experts call such dying paradoxical undressing.
It's when a body can't wait to tear off her clothes.
When it comes to love, what does anybody know?

ANNAGHMAKERRIG

I

Who do you think you are sleet spat
Against the pane with characteristic
Originality and what do you think
You're doing here her husband swayed
As much as saying give it up?

I have been chosen, I am staying,
Hibernating at this heady
Latitude. Please, just go away
And let me linger, seep like daylight,
Gnaw like nightmare at the afternoon.

This will be my sleeping chamber
Where tomorrow I will wake
To color, someone else's scheme:
Gray, wine, navy, tangerine,
Chartreuse, harmonies unknown,

And lace floating on a film
Like breath on glass, mahogany
So polished with another's tears
The doily is a face in it,
A face, perhaps, from Carrickmacross.

I am not worthy, I intone,
And rub a long, doubting finger
Dustless over marble. Silver frames
Prop lives up on the mantle, two maids
In muslin mobcaps rutched with giggles.

II

Who am I that I should be so given
Amplified a quiet like the roar
Of the equator spanned inside the brain,
That suddenly I should be fit to hear
Everything, the ladylike adjustment
Of the smoldering coals inside the grate
Dying gracefully, rain against the casement,
And below that unmistakable scrape
Of hunger, someone scuttling in the dark,
Skimming the surface only, then the trudge
Back up. I count each step, each breath, the creak
Inquisitive outside my door, my blood
Drumming to a half-heard wail. These walls are thin,
A tympanum, then seas antipodean.

III

There has to be a plot.
Even here there's smut
In cyberspace. It's three
O'clock. The sun is weary
Already of its trek through ozone
Wastes we once called heaven.
Things are under chthonic
Wraps. Black plastic
Everywhere. Cylinders
Of hay incinerated
Tidbits charred. The cries
Of cut grass sealed in body
Bags rolled up upon
Themselves laid out at random
In the cloned green grass:
Promises, promises, promises.

And the bloated, leprous guts
Of earthworm nissen huts
That incubate albino
Mushroom growths.
The airplane hanger barns
That ululate alarm.
Unnatural silence. Pong
Of chicken shit. The bomb
In deepest Monaghan.
Capons and the arms run.
They snip their cords, you know,
Then play the radio
To brooding hypochondriacs
Who don't let out a squawk.

And the black plastic duvets
That asphyxiate the hay

In bed that doesn't breathe
A word, the margins heave
But do not move. The chest
Constricted, ballasted,
Impaled like cloud on bones,
Huge, Amazonian stones
In garish fertilizer
Sacks. They've only realized
They are lost, the chemical
Colors of exotic, tropical
Birds flapping manically
In Monaghan in panic.

Incest everywhere.
Eyes that cross in mid-air
Trying to string two words
Together which converge
At last inside the barrel
Of a gun trying to kill
Some time. Spent cartridges
In ditches. How many partridge
Does it take even to maim
The past? You take your aim.
You shoot your wad, then walk
Away trying to slough off
Guilt. At least the yokes
These days can take a joke,
Splitting their lurid latex
Sides guffawing. Sex
A ride on mangled, plastic
Wings. The swan is sick
And tired of it. Plumage
Littering the ditches.

It came wavering,
A sudden apparition,

Thin shanks and florid
Faces, men or gods,
Buoyed on a sea of beagles,
Foolish animals
In well-pressed gabardine
And emerald velveteen,
Attired in proper habits,
Jackets, jodhpurs, helmets,
Boots. Dressed to kill
And heading home, a little
Tired, a little pissed,
Regenerate to Newbliss.

And a mad, white rabbit
Zigzags across acid
Green, the empty screen
When I am on my own
Again, a dogged finger
Chasing a psychotic cursor.

And the fox? Virtual
Reality, as real
As it can get, caught
In the apocalyptic
Glare of headlights, stretched
As far as truth permits
From the unseen star
At the tip of its tail to the curve
Of its aerodynamic snout,
Spine fused with purpose,
Bushy brush emphatic,
Delicate jaws open
To the bitter end, abstraction
Setting off each lethal
Canine. Every bristle
Of its muck encrusted fur

Calibrated, tapered
Like a tooth. The point to bite
And tear and chew and grind.
The miracle, survival,
The original vicious circle.

IV

It was better than being pregnant or crazy: tiptoes
Whispers, smiles, a retinue of mothers
Leaving me free to wander corridors
Embossed with words, flocked with innuendo.

I refused, however, every knock, hand, voice
Beseeching me. I cleaned like a maniac
My own room, sweat staining the antimacassars
And the anemic pages that needed exercise.

This is the art I'd never learned to others'
Satisfaction, down on my knees in dirt,
In regular, rhythmic motions exposing guilt,
Using a toothbrush to get into the cracks and corners.

I spurn all effort made on my behalf.
Every hair for my sake out of place, frowns
Lining faces as I write, all the fallen
Arches and beyond the wall the muffled laughter.

An anorexic of the senses I aspire
To an innocence as thin as a page in profile,
As blank as the face of my unspeakable vileness,
Laboring for starched, impeccable order.

V

A verdict from the past: you have no voice.
The fish-bone notes sticking, a gagging noise.

Better to hold your whisht. Learn to listen.
Let the others scale sheer air. Be their witness.

However, high on this hill my new family
Coaxes words back to the breast of melody.

They will not hear of my polite refusals.
Everyone a genius. Everyone a fool.

My mother's mood suddenly lifting. Anger
Cooled by the clever breeze of Cole Porter.

Ankle socks and wedgies, a housedress in a floral
Print, a red bandanna turban over pincurls.

Fly with me. Come fly. Come fly away.
Peru. Bombay. Let's do it. Birds and bees.

I get no kick. I lie. I did. But there is nothing
Under my skin now that I am singing.

Deadbolt rhymes that shunt and lock in place,
A little kiss, a sudden slap in the face.

Intoxicating rhythm, Three AM
Tirades smoothed by a love that's merely human,

Nightingales are girls again. This muteness
Is reversed. A tongue at last. Sweet mutiny

And power. Come night, the knife and fork lie down
And song, like smoke, rises from its bower

Stretching at the bar of standards, oldies
Out-of-key and out-of-tune. Family.

Even the wine label sings its own hosannas
To the grape: Carignan, Grenache and Syrah.

Everything converted, saved. The table
Levitates. And I have the voice of an angel.

VI

Bolt the creaky shutters from the inside tight.
Night can ooze and seep and moonlight eat
Like maggots deep into the sleeper's alabaster flesh
Coffined in her dreams, hair and fingernails
Still breathing. Time to batten down the brain.

Stoke the fire. Build the structure high
Enough to make you shed unnecessary
Layers. You are protected by the light
Around your body, the erratic lick
Of flame, your wicked, heliotropic nature.

Worse, a fire-eater. Crime that you were made for,
Sucking heat, quenching danger in your wet
Interior. The entire fire curling like a crotch,
Power stolen from our one and only source. The center
Shifts. Your bones becomes a funeral pyre.

VII

Pretend that this is silence,
The self-effacing breeze of prayer,
The taste of pure gratitude.

Not just to be fed
Until the exigent blood
Breathes a sigh of relief

But until every bud,
A blossom on the tongue,
Sits up to the sun and opens.

Every brain cell bathed
In awe registers the presence
In the room of genius.

Endlessly inventive, toothsome
Company, who or what,
I wonder, will it be tonight?

Neighbours with the tact
And passion of the perfect, smooth
Unhegemonic sauce.

Perfect matches. Souls so satisfied
They're tempted to depart
The flesh and feel no loss.

A consommé so clear
It's an epiphany, the humble
Spud steamed to a broad smile.

One al dente surprise
After another, the integrity
Of broccoli, mange tout, and friends.

The wit of fêta nuggets,
Radish flakes and pine nuts
Folded into red lettuce

Leaves as lightly dressed
As stimulating talk,
The vocabulary of greens.

Steak that has been seared
To such hermetic perfection
It begs the knife for mercy.

The mellow belly of a soufflé
(Ironic to be ravished
When you thought the lid was down).

Exquisite food, the kind
To take with you into the tomb,
Nourishment for the hereafter.

Dessert after dessert. Velvet
Chocolate mousse, the queen
Of puddings, Doreen's apple tart.

Night after night, delight
After delight, eternal pleasure.
A body wasn't made for this.

Panting toward the finish
Line, I must confess, I almost
Lost the run of myself.

VIII

A gravitation toward the weight
Of things, a man's body pressing
On your brain as flat as sickness,
The unconsciousness of ironing.

A clean sheet dreaming over
Winter waves, the chaste precision
Of the iron. Vertiginous on deck.
The wedge expanding in your wake.

Nobody can claim a part of you
In there, the deep, smooth, pristine
Drowning of demands, desire, the bell
They press that's wired to your skin.

A little kiss, a grope. You're up
Against the wall, up to your eyeballs
In the frothing coal. Your whole body
Treacherous. The sin. The sea. The bell.

The pale mistress with her shoulder
Pads and shadow pains, the beaded
Gardenia on her breast. The master
In his boudoir with his boys.

The noise of other people's lives.
The silence of your own. Midnight.
Relief. Turning over a new leaf.
Your white diary and body.

IX

The eye scavenges
In gaps, seeks solutions
Sideways scanning hedgerows,
Reason's inexorable
Green, desperate for a speck
Of sense, so the brown trout
Muscling its way
Upstream spots in its taut
Skin capsule colored
Like the frothing river
And our doubts, dappled,
Dun, an answer lying
On the under-surface
Of its thoughts where sun-
Light falling on the onyx
Water breaks its neck
On impact, giving up
The ghost, becomes the tune
We can't quite put our finger
On diluting as we
Walk nameless through
The fading afternoon
Filtering the facts

So I saw my opportunity:
Two doors side by side,
Upright in a field,
Victorian spouses, out-
Of-context, out-to-pasture,
Opening on nothing
In particular,
Some droll farmer's desperate
Joke—in one door
And out the other, both,

The out-of-doors, no
Enclosure, no cement
Or stone, just lines, a black
Box domesticating
Green, the involuntary
Eye's idea of home.

Or those wisps of fancy,
Feathers, curlicues
Of rusty wire, twigs
And twine in petrol blue,
The warp and woof of walking
Woven through the iron
Railings of a gate. Predators
And pooka kept a bay
Alike. To kill one bird
Is to locate the other.

Winter, scorched and bleached,
Leaves as pale as parchment,
Thin as faith, seed pods,
Stalks of straw. The word
Is chaff and I, a stranger
To these parts, haven't
Even the names by which
Summer is remembered.

I note them by their sere
Particulars, the gold leaf,
Fresco flakes of dead
Petals, summer's scabs,
The bony, stripped, umbrella
Pedestal of wild
Fennel, perhaps. How many bees
Have sipped from that believing
Face wide-open to the sun?

An exact, exacting season.
Sketched in sepia
And washed by rain.
Tears are appropriate.
And yet the closer to the ground
You get the more the separate
Stars, reflected in
The bog, come out and glow
Paprika, mustard, moss,
Obsidian and plum
Stygian and rich,
Wet bark breathing.

Reiteration of design.
Crystalline like bracken,
Lichen, frost, or guilt,
Lines that take their shape
From palimpsests of seasons,
Former seasons and the sun.

Phalluses or severed
Tongues in lavender,
Ambiguous and mute,
Catkins dangling from dark
Branches either desiccated
Or about to burst.

Ripples of a fern,
An animal whose stripes
Are silent in the tiger
Maple, arctic waves
Made eloquent in ice.

Diseased and webbed the feet
Of maple leaves with turtle

Melanoma spots. The mulch
Of drumlin after drumlin
Rotting in the brain.

Sesshu Toyo thinking
In degrees of ink
Made his landscape come up
Darker and darker still
In the cursive style,
The way a God might sketch
The perfect world in haste,
The way a victim wakes up
Gradually from coma,
Nascent mountains yawning
Out of gray infinity,
A few, bold calligraphic
Strokes, the black slashes
Of a crow flapping.

The tangled, tragic skein
Of winey briars beaded
After rain, the human tears
Of legions of brilliant, bloodless
Metaphysicians, ocular
And oval, some balancing
On thorns, elongating
As I watch their steady
Progress downward heavy
With an undue knowing.
They have been thinking this
For years, the pain of waiting.
This is their last, pellucid
Drop, diamond bright,
Deliquescent as the flesh.
I would have to stand forever
Here in one place, learn

The name of every face
To mark faithfully
Their falling through the barbed-
Wire of these final hours.

X

It was even a little comical now that it was
Visible: lust's jumble from beyond the wall
Of broken sleep poking every which way from the pit,
Sitting up at table like a fat baby in his lap.

The thick pipe with a lip like a foreskin. The swollen
Sack protected by a velvet membrane sewn
From some other woman's blood. The udder sucking
The stem the way satyr fur attaches to a shank.

I couldn't take my eyes off it. The ring around
The root primitively carved. The teethmarks
Of a shark embedded in a nipple, soft cloth
Besotted with wood, tooth for tooth, stitching for chipping.

An old, Viking couple huddled by a fire. Mud
And wattle, bracken insulation, all that exists
Between them and extinction. The woman is unraveling
Her ball of thoughts. Woodchips flare around his crotch.

Repeated patterns of the everyday recovered
From the dark. Shards of pottery and porphyry,
Spindle whorls and pins of bone, antler combs
With teeth so fine they are bodies we are given.

XI

(The list tacked to the inside of the door of the old linen closet.)
House Linens Annaghmakerrig October 1889

16 Dinner tablecloths
70 Dinner napkins
12 Fish napkins
18 Linen sheets
18 Twilled sheets
12 Plain linen pillow covers
18 Kitchen cloths
6 Round towels
30 Glass cloths
24 Dusters
4 Hall cloths
4 Dishing cloths
8 Bolster covers
36 Servants' sheets
24 Servants' pillowcases
4 Tray cloths
4 Teatable cloths
36 Best towels
12 Common towels
36 Servants' towels
12 Best blankets
12 Single blankets
12 Toilet covers
12 Bath towels

PART THREE

After Snow

All night it raged. Come daylight it
Was over, washed and ironed, starched,
Crystal and a linen tablecloth,
So clean, as my mother would say, you could eat
Off the floor. With every step I scorch
Creation. My body is too heavy for this earth.

ONLY RENTING

Of course, I know by now
They must have seemed vulgar,
Our showy displays, the instant
Gratification of the poor,

Annuals and shrill geraniums
Standing up for us on a rented
Sill, brash petunias bending
Over backwards for some sun.

My mother kept the budget,
Reeled our laundry out
And in on a long, taut pulley line,
The only ends that met.

I should have pitied her,
Leaning out that high window,
Breasting the cold like a bird,
Her fingers stiff as clothespins.

A windowbox in summer
Was my mother's pride and joy,
Her only pride, her only joy,
It seemed. She watered it with sweat

And rushed around the kitchen
In a dingy bra and slip,
Hauling off, giving me a slap
For giving her such lip.

If I'm my mother's enemy,
I'd reason, as a flower might,
The sky must be jealous of my breath,
The earth begrudge my footsteps.

I'd sit on the stoop and sob
And sulk, self-pity choked
On self-aggrandizement. Even
The lawn belonged to someone else.

Every blade and every tear
But what was most unfair
Were those old-fashioned roses,
Flesh on the bones of a trellis.

The light inside it trembled
Chapel pale and scented, impossible
To say or separate my shame
From the sheer act of breathing.

It took my breath away, dawn
Pink back as though nothing
Had happened, buds packed tight,
Like a baby's intact mouth.

I've not forgotten. The spot
Still smarts; but those tears that flowed
As freely as the roses tumbled,
They still belong to someone else.

ENTROPY

I might have been adopted,
The research that intense,
A particle so light even I
Assumed I had no mass.

I tried to live my life
Light years from the source.
Danger was up close,
Distance a red and angry star.

Now I am back. A law
Of physics willing this collapse
Of matter into chaos,
Rediscovering I have a mother.

DREAMERS

My mother's standing pointing at the sky in a dream,
"Can you see it, there?" I hear her cry in a dream.

My head is in the clouds like yours. I know it now,
But you're the one to blame. I'm in a quandary, in a dream.

Give me the blank banked tall with vague immensities,
I too am racing, drifting, floating high in a dream.

I will never see things as you'd have me do,
Blood logic. Madness I defy in a dream.

Up there it's white, opaque like gauze the thought won't hold;
We fall through space discover we can fly in a dream.

Bears and whales and galleons. Heaven has a face,
The lover which we fail to place, identify in a dream.

The dead can speak. The sea divides. I am the bride.
And I don't need to find a reason why in a dream.

Insistence weighs but you must see we can't agree.
God will weep if we see eye-to-eye in a dream.

A mother and a daughter shouldn't be the same.
Panthers pace like jealousy that boundary in a dream.

Yes, I look like you. The mirror has your mouth.
It bit me once and now I am twice shy in a dream.

A life spent sucking at the source, the planetary curve
Of cheek and breast synonymous, you and I in a dream.

She is the judge, the jury too. I stand accused
Of crimes I half-remember and deny in a dream.

The stone will budge. You will be free when you, Peggy,
Grasp the solid truth you too will die in a dream.

MY SHADOW

—for Meg

Her head is in the clouds.
She comes up nearly to my elbow.
Everywhere I go
Questions follow.

Where do they go
The girls without the mirrors?
Knowing what she doesn't know,
A born philosopher.

She is watching as I watch
My image floss and brush my teeth,
Her little chin a judgment
With the incline of a truth.

I am in the land of symmetries.
My shimmering familiar
Locks me with her magnet eyes,
But why my gadfly ponders.

Every night the mime, the dance,
The bedtime minuet
My infamous impatience
Spattering the glass with quicklime spit.

On the other side of ice my twin,
Elusive, pliant,
Rigid with her one insistent question
Needles vision snow-blind.

Thank God for distractions:
Hot chocolate sloshing in its sockets,

Balancing a tray of questions
Fished from her deep, secret pocket.

Why are emeralds green
And what gives telephones their ring?
Do you know what I mean?
Granny, are you listening?

Being Weaned

I take care of myself.
On the deck in striped pajamas,
Having breakfast, sipping

Assam tea. Suddenly
A phone call cuts the silence
Like a fresh Pain au Levain,

Sliced at unnatural, even
Intervals, not by hand
But by a cruel machine.

Could it be that someone
Needs me? Maybe a dire
Emergency at this unearthly

Hour? Unfortunately not.
Funny how we know
The sound of our own ring,

Its tenor, timing, pitch,
One cry guttural, another
More an urgent screech,

The way a mother knows
Her offspring from the rest
Wrapped in identical flannelette,

Wailing down a corridor, too many
Doors, an institution, our first,
Separated night on earth.

A MODEST SERVICE

Your lotus blossom hand in mine,
The two of us are weary geishas
Who have given up at last on hate
And love, all for the sake of the mime.

Mother and daughter, we may not color
Our lips madder or ghost our skin
Matte, immaculate, but we are trying
To make-up, to smooth things over.

I admit neglect became an art
With me: the sadistic fit of symmetries,
Tit for tat, but even I, as you say,
As hard as nails can have a heart,

Or in lieu of that generous organ a limit
To the suffering I'll inflict, even
To get even. Your brittle, bird bones
Once had weight, heaved, levered, hit;

But that was of no moment when,
Sitting in that waiting room waiting
For results, I saw your broken wings
Flapping in your lap, your sad talons

And my shame exposed. You've been alone
Too long and I orphaned by anger.
This is not a cure; it's just a manicure.
I'm not about to file and polish pain.

Just whose hand is it? Mutilated,
Jagged, ribbed and split, unregenerate,
These nails are mine, their high instep
Also mine. For the first time I see it.

You begged me to paint you blowzy
As a poppy, but taught me not to tell
A lie. I chose instead a mountain laurel
Beige closer to what's natural. "I'm sorry,"

I say, "I have to leave. Let them dry
Thoroughly, eat more, please, and take your new
Medicine." All you reply is "Thank you,"
As you stand in the doorway waving good-bye.

TIMMY'S TABLE

Your kohl emboldened eyes are meeting my dark circles,
Dread of my only child made-up as the pale angel

Of death. It's a black-and-white snapshot of the two of us opposite
Each other at this very table, joined and separated

By three feet of pine, which remains unfinished. It can come up
Bone anytime, you ten years ago, with plain soap

And water. To this day in one of my penitential humors
I'll get out that hard bristle brush you know well and scour

The hell, the life and soul, out of the soft wood. All my weight
Behind the regular, circular motions. Grease and dirt

Fly in my furious wake like flesh from a starving frame.
I'm left like someone on a death fast seeing the grain,

The stuff from which it's made, for the first time, flame
Singeing deal, your cropped, punk, root-dark, platinum

Head, a duckling or a martial eagle, the shock of your skull
In profile, gaunt features struck immortal on a wall.

Your deathwish was as abstract as a shadow cast on sand,
Immediate as its bleached skeleton, your hipbones hands

Beseeching an angry sun. I wanted to be the kind of mother
Who has the answers, but I was looking in a warped mirror

Of myself: hyped, reversed, macabre. You'd become a blond,
But blinding like a movie star, punished yourself to the son

I'd thought I coveted. All my sins cupped in a clavicle
Fragile as Belleek, that dent in your wrist like a salt cellar.

This should have been a groaning board coming down with love,
Instead its knots were bitter nipples, wormwood dugs.

Unnatural weaning, I'd pick at a knot as I still can do a scab,
Search my mop for split ends, worry the body scholastic.

Talk and more talk. Fed up, I'd start looking out an airplane
Window at the various and beautiful topography of pain,

Wavy ledges like sand dunes disappearing into a too blue
Ocean below. I wanted but I knew I couldn't follow you

Down, dive to a depth where no one could survive,
Loving you as life itself, fearing you'd eat me alive.

Paralyzed, transfixed, I was witnessing a vision of the virgin
Beating her sinless, gold-leaf breast flat as an icon.

Artifact and artist both, for months you'd carved your flesh
With gleaming blades of self-control, regarded your own breath

As an esthetic effect, an icy stream racing over a chalk bed,
Limestone karst beatified by one, perfect orchid.

A minimalist gone berserk, you'd come to see beauty only
In the macerated, alpine waif not the womanly peony.

Who had set such strict standards, fed you all the wrong
Words? You were so thin, when you'd turn away in scorn,

It was a total eclipse. You'd seen, I feared, the black center
Of my eyes the second after you were born, charred forever

By that freezing knowledge. I remember watching a stranger cut
The cord and you reeling off dazzling into your own, separate

Orbit. It was a miracle. The sun in its full radiance coming out
Again. Hunger like sweet tears or a tide recovering my daughter.

And the table survived. I hauled it and you across the Atlantic,
All my furniture and guilt (something I'd neglected to pack?).

You went back to your father, left me staring at a sea of prairie grass,
Me and whomever I faced. There were days when it seemed a vast

Distance: breaking up and breaking down, coming home
Again, separation after separation, from you and all you'd known,

Your own, your only life. This humble table had been sent on a train
Up to Dublin, along with six hand-sugawned chairs, your inheritance,

A wedding present from your grandfather, your father's father, Timmy,
Who'd bought them and a marriage bed, alas far too narrow, in Tralee

Then dispatched the lot with a message attached, "Long life and health
To ye." Unappreciated at the time, it's blessings like these we feed off

For life. Sitting here in my new life, in the New World, with a new
Friend, chin set at that acute angle, it's you I'm talking to.

All it takes is a call, a disembodied voice, and once again I'm filled
With dread. The difference now is love has also proved insatiable.

Ruth

I. The Name

It has always sounded dark
To me and natural, yews and roots
With blood-black clots of humus still
Attached, a uterus, a bruise,
A wound, the truth, a vulnerable
Vowel between soft consonants
Like lips. To say it is to taste
The bitterness of rue, or women,
Know the sorrow of this earth,
Perennial, profuse as sin,
Mint, golden seal or yarrow.
Stemmed and veined, it is complex,
A species on its own, and yet
Common as a weed, this name, Ruth,
For certain human pain. It has
A history and properties;
It sprouts paradox like leaves
With two distinctly different sides
As people have, and more. It is the cure
That grows beside the bane, dock leaves
Soothing and spontaneous as rain
On a summer day, a sudden shower
Of true forgiveness, unexpected
Goodness nestling into nettle
Spears. It is my mother's name.

II. GENEALOGY

The patriarchal thumb rubs
An unguent liturgy, chrism
Of oblivion, into the newborn's brow,
Pulsing with trust. The helpless drape
Of pristine lace and linen is
A promise. We are christened into dust.

Genealogy unfurls. It's only
Natural. Family. Yahweh.
Every sacred branch a son,
Canopy of generations, open
To the blaze of revelation,
Covenanted seed and star,
Each oblique angle
Upward pre-ordained. Boaz
Begat Obed begat Jesse
Begat David. Elaborate
Of plan, above and underground,
The necessary root system
(Mothers, daughters, sisters)
Anchoring the green edifice.
The lie is intricate and vast,
Equal to the visible, the chosen
Truth. We are from whence we came.

III. SNAPSHOT

I see you standing like a birch
In winter, bare of hope, abstracted
As an old, scratched photograph, staring
Out the window at the kitchen
Sink, the water in the basin
Turning cold, the light dilute,
Your hands immersed to an unnatural
White, magnified and alien.

IV. FAMILIES

What do we know of your elusive
Ancestress, the chaste Moabitess,
So protected by the words
Of men her motivations are
Unspoken? Boaz ordering his men-
Servants not to molest the radiant
Stranger in their midst. All those pro-
Hibitions against incest, lids
Placed on a fiercely boiling pot, pimping
Mothers and the blood in riot.
You knew what you were at, the protection
Racket it is only smart to crook
The knee at, paying with your tits
And ass for the interest of a decent
Man, you who had seen it all
Before, the paw clamped up against
Your jaw. Each black, insolent hair
A visible reason to be silent.
The words of protest flare then die,
Swallowed back into the body,
A trick you had to master early.

V. The Search

How many times must we be asked
To forget the map of reason as we
Know it, the sewing kit inside
The jug up on the shelf, where else,
The scar that beats beneath the scatter-
Rug, strategically placed? Domestic
Logic. We love the best the child
Who hurts us most and understand
The exodus to stranger lands
Than us, the need to be bereft
As chaff, yet gravid with a purpose,
To know again a hunger keen
As steel, the gleaming, whetted edge,
And stand alone amidst a foreign
Order, row upon burnished row.

I have seen a woman worshipped for her face,
Its strict, iconic features and impassive
Gaze, rampage through a moth-proof
Cedar chest searching for disease.

I have known a mother mad as Job
Perpetuate injustice, bang
Against the drum of rage, flesh
Of her flesh, for an answer from it.

And I have seen a daughter dis-
Appear into a distant wish
To die, immaculate and honed
To bone, the skin of her uniqueness
Stretched to a spun-glass web of hate,
Talk of what she will and will not
Eat, the gauze of mother-daughter
Love, that knit of wills, balanced

On a knife edge, every fatal thread
In jeopardy, reason frayed,
Unselvaged anger on display,
Implausible behavior, except
From one who's seen the star, been chosen
For the altar, her mantel woven
From the finest gauge despair,
Lying bare on exposed shoulder blades.

VI. TRANSGRESSION

My mother fell in love with a god
-Damned Irish Catholic, penniless
To boot. And that was that. The war
Was on. She lived at home, like a sentry
High on Prospect Hill. When her Yankee
Father, however, saw the stone, tiny,
To be fair, as a star we know
Is there but rarely see, that man,
Simmering with others' sins, kicked
His only, far too lovely daughter
Out of his house for good. She packed
Her heartache in a cardboard suitcase,
Traipsed in high heels and a flimsy
Dress five miles to a friend's house
Down a dirt road through the needle's eye
Of night at the end of which the future
Shone, it and the man-in-the-moon.
She took instruction, went to mass,
Abandoned the familiar hymns,
Like saying good-bye to lullabies,
For the damp of stone and swoon of incense,
Heady as sex. On a cold-sweat day
In June they married. My father was
On three-day leave. I was conceived
In a cabin on a beach in Florida.
Back home alone, bowed like the belly
Of a hammock, she moved across
The tracks to a cold-water flat in the Polish
District. Neither fish nor fowl, she had
Her baby on a bitter day in early
March. And it befell she had
A daughter. Neither family visited. I howled
Incessantly from colic. She walked
The floor shivering with me, the same

Few yards of threadbare carpet, circular
And endless, as that road, and yet
Her baby's eyes, such sweet forget-
Me-nots, shone like the sea her hubby
Rode upon pacifically. Suddenly
The war was over; he came home;
They fought incessantly; and I
Grew up. That apartment hovers still,
Airborne before words, as pools
Of color float before a newborn
Infant's gaze. It had a kitchen
Floor pitched at an angle so
Precipitate, I'm told, I walked
At nine months old. There was no choice
In the matter. I never looked back.
And that, I like to say, was that.

VII. HOME AND DRY

A woman can love the idea of conclusion
In a way a man may witness only
In his dreams. Standing on the edge
Of a huge ocean, his toes curling
In the coolness. Ruth elected
Barrenness, Naomi's dried pod
Womb, scoured by successive
Losses to a curved, perfect
Emptiness echoing to past
Disturbances the way sand takes
Its contours from the wind but other-
Wise an end to the interminable
Process, stasis, choice, a place
In which to hear your own voice.

VIII. The Mother

My mother's mother disappeared into other
People's whispers about cancer;
But my mother's step-mother took steps
To leave abuse behind forever
In Revere, Massachusetts. Riding westward
In a blur of terror. Would he follow
Her again? Could she make it on
Her own? Transgressing the tribe in order
To survive. Pulling up the possible
Name of an employer like a ragged scrap
Of courage tucked into her pocket,
Finding in time that even fear
Can leave, the days becoming clear
As rainwater methodically collected
In a barrel, the usual routine,
The same eternal round, a prism
Not a prison when the effort
Is for others, a detached
Sensation, a privilege to lay
The vivid threads of tasks out parallel
And crossed, to touch them and arrange
Them thus and so, making the day.
It was a miracle. This and that she met
A man deliberate as Boaz,
Married, raised another woman's
Issue as her own, with greater
Grace because they were her choice,
A family given to her barren days.
There was no room left to complain.
She became the virgin sprayed
By faith, Naomi wondering at Ruth,
The danger in her young will.
She was loss reconstellated, inner
Light to a womb so far blind

To creation. Ruth was weedy, stringy,
Rampant, wild, her head the tow
Of dandelion fluff, volatile
And scatterbrained. She glowed freedom.

IX. MASTER AND SERVANT

Tipsy with prosperity, sprawled
And snoring on the threshing floor,
Boaz was so exhausted he dreamed
The day's labor over, ghost
Harvesting his crop, floating
In a topaz haze, groping his way
Dazed through corridors without
Answers, stalks so thickly sewn
He walked among his sins, reaping
His yield, the fields' ripe confusion,
Gathering the sheaves forever
Of his deeds, a widower winnowing
His past, the seep of pain through aging
Limbs. Suddenly there was a woman
Lying at his feet, in fact, on them.
She was more resplendent even than acres
Of glinting grain or the flesh of an ear
Of corn freshly shucked by an expert,
Deftly in a few quick strokes,
The plump kernels and the amber
Skin a vision, hair so fine it must be
Hidden and forbidden to any other
Hands except a husband's. That body was
A prophecy, a shaft of nakedness
Across his unprotected bow,
Exposed by the bold Moabitess.

Like a wide-necked, full-hipped silver
Ewer, as beautiful as it is
Serviceable, waiting to be
Filled up to the brim with well-
Water, an exiled woman seems
An ideal vessel for a man,
For the gush of his hyperbole.

The truth is Ruth had spunk. Knew
Her luck. She was a pragmatist
Who heard the siren swish of uncut
Promise in the near distance.
She also knew for some reason
Intimately as the contours
Of her sandal that man, the master.

Yes, she could handle him, witness
Boaz ordering his men to strew
Her path with fallen ears of corn,
Flowers in the footsteps of a queen.
Every day Ruth gleaned more and more.
But she was honest in her dealings
Reaping only for her needs,
Hers and Naomi's. Her spine was supple
As a willow standing out
Among the multitude, men
And women bending on a swelling
Ocean, the days unbroken swaying
Motion, obeying someone else's
Will, blushing to the ticklish
Brush of rough, tufts of grain
Under her skirt, feeling the firmness
Of a corn baton, shaped, it seemed
To fit a woman's palm: curve
For curve her touch was sure. She walked
Away from the labor flushed and spent,
A nation in her apron and six
Measures of barley for Naomi.

X. RUTHLESS

You step out of the car. I am tempted
To say, "Good-bye, Ruth" and not
"Mom" or "Mother" for the air
This winter day is clear and you are
Etched for me as ordinary, an "old
Lady," as you say, returning
Home from an outing with a daughter
Who was doing her duty. For impunity
I follow you into the kitchen.
"I can't linger," I say, "It's getting
Darker earlier these days,
Besides, you know, I have to go
To work tomorrow." By the way,
That front tooth that you've lost. I ought
To give you one of mine, you
Who gave me breath. I have excuses
To spare. I used them to escape
This house and now they are all I have.
An eye for an eye, a tooth for a tooth.
"What will you do now," I ask, "after
I have gone?" "Oh, I have
A lot to do, the usual, roll
My hair up, set the table, take
A bath, do some reading, and tomorrow
I'll get up and after breakfast
Start again to put an order
On this house. Since your father's death,
I don't know where I am. His
Papers, clothes, the lawyer's bills.
Don't you worry about me, dear, you
Worry about yourself." Last
Night I looked you up. You are
A common noun as well as a proper
One. You are the special sadness

One can harbor for one's own
Shortcomings, the magnanimity
Of God, if God were flawed. As for me,
I try my best to be ruthless.

XI. SEDUCTION

It was the child, her famished chat
The way she leaned into her dour
Father like a tree trunk that
Had caught your eye, you with the Atwater
Brats in tow, no more than flowers
To the sun was George Lampson's
Thought, his own wan daughter
Propped up by his side, abandoned
By her mother's cancer. Since Hattie's
Death he'd been bereft. What to do
With Ruth? He let her ride the trollies
With him but he knew that he could do
With a woman. The boys were still at home.
They too could use you. You were wary.
You had had enough of charm
And cuffs and curses, didn't want to marry
Again, necessarily. You'd watched your marriage
Rushing past like all the unknown
Towns beyond Boston and the ravaged
Face reflected in the train
Window worrying what it
Would do in Westfield when the green
Transition across Massachusetts
Ended you'd be on your own.
But hadn't that been always so?
Your own mother leaving just
As you arrived. It felt as though
A body simply could not trust
A soul. Your stepmother had taught
You what a mother ought to be:
Everything your stepmother was not.
You even sensed how mother-hungry
The most ordinary families
Can be, even could imagine

Children somewhere so lonely
They would suck gladly milk from a stone.
You advertised your services,
Became a nursemaid in the richest
Home in town. The children were harmless.
You had your own room plus the best
Of food. You had fallen on your feet.
They even took you on vacation
With them so as not to be without
Their Dora. Until you'd left for Maine,
It really hadn't dawned on George
A day might come when you would not
Alight, your instep boldly arched,
Your back strong and supple, straight
As a birch, at the corner of Elm and Broad.
That slow man acted in a flash
The way his temper worked if roused
And drove all night to reach
Monhegan by the morning. Stars tumbled
Around Ruthie's head, bulleting
Through pitch. She sat tight in the rumble
Seat for much of the way, her hair fast
To her head the way grass is threaded
Over stone when spring's in spate
Or the way a bird's intelligent feathers
Close its mind to all but flight,
The airtight fantasy of no
Body at all, this element
Called mother that she knew would hold
Her always. She had no idea what it meant.
Except years later when she traced that old
Scar. She saw her mother, for she was
Her mother now, inside out unfold.
Dying does that to us, lays
The body out for all to see
Us scars and all. It was another

Bout of cancer, but Ruth traced
That woman's secrets like the rivers
Of her own inchoate past.
Suddenly she knew the path.
Start nearly on the inside of a wrist,
Then up the arm and underneath
An armpit, straight across the absence
Of a breast, the other one,
The armpit, arm and wrist. The sense
Of it was radical, un-
Bearable almost. All those trees,
The night, the journey, shadows
Bending, tucking safely babies
In, were in that room, the ghosts
At last prepared to speak the truth.
That night she learned to see that scar
As something other than an old wound.
It seemed, she fought the thought, a zipper
Set in finest crepe now frayed
And yet her mother was full of hope
Though even flatter to the naked
Eye, like an envelope
Of antique parchment that had opened
Unreservedly, disclosed
Its contents freely, organs, glands
And blood and now was sealing its soul.

XII. GLEANING AMONG THE SHEAVES

The lights are out. The door is locked,
Double-locked by guilt. The bolt
Is drawn across my tears but still
I hear that sound, the inimitable lilt
Of pleasure, swish and hum of late
Summer, skirts and scythes, the aching
Cadences of twilight, women
Coming to the well and leaving
Full, balancing their bright
Burdens level as they navigate
The sands, their long, golden hands
With palms upturned, the balm
Of evening cupped. We make this pilgrimage
To a mirage, a faint wavering
And tinkling. We drink and are
Refreshed by simply living, though you,
As you like to say, may be dead by morning.
Each of us by now, I trust,
Is up in bed, fast asleep,
Swaying to our separate dreams. Two women
Completely on our own at last.
Not just gleaning after the reapers
But gleaning among the sheaves themselves.